T0069123

SELECTED POEMS OF
RAINER MARIA
RILKE
TRANSLATION AND INTRODUCTION BY DAVID YOUNG

SELECTED POEMS OF

RAINER MARIA
RILKE

TRANSLATION AND INTRODUCTION BY DAVID YOUNG

THE BOOK
OF FRESH BEGINNINGS

THE FIELD TRANSLATION SERIES 20

Publication of this book was made possible by support from
the Ohio Arts Council and the National Endowment for the
Arts.

Library of Congress Cataloging in Publication Data

Rilke, Rainer Maria (translation and introduction by
   David Young)
THE BOOK OF FRESH BEGINNINGS: SELECTED POEMS
(The FIELD Translation Series v. 20)

Copyright © 1994 by Oberlin College
LC: 93-087297
ISBN: 0-932449-68-1
        0-932440-67-3 (paperback)

CONTENTS

III   Requiem for a Friend (1908)   65

IV   from *Sonnets to Orpheus* (1923)   77

INTRODUCTION

Telling Rilke's story, by way of introducing a selection of his poems, is a fairly tricky business. This poet was a solitary figure, atypical even as an artist, who shrank from many of the ties — family, nation, politics — that defined his contemporaries; at the same time he was also, in many ways, a mirror of his era. Cosmopolitan, cultivating aristocratic patronage, taking the whole of Europe as his spiritual homeland, he exemplified many of the best characteristics of European culture before the First World War. Which way you see him depends somewhat upon your distance and focus, and on the cut of your paradigm. And while the twin curves of his life and career may not be altogether characteristic of other great modern writers, they tell us a good deal about changes that took place as the nineteenth century gave way to the twentieth and about the way art responded to those changes — in some cases reinforcing them, in others resisting and protesting them.

So many statements about Rilke require contradiction or qualification as soon as they are made; those corrections then require their own readjustments, so that our insights and reactions zig and zag. Rilke was married and had a daughter, but he found he could not live with his family. Nevertheless, he regularly wrote long, marvelous letters to his wife. His language and nationality were German (Prague Bohemian, more precisely), but he detested the time he had to spend in Germany, especially during the First World War, and greatly preferred France, Italy, Scandinavia and Switzerland. For all that, his ties with German culture, especially German romanticism, are deep and significant. And if we say that Rilke was not someone who sat around in salons with symbolists or in cafes with Dadaists and futurists, we must immediately add that he was profoundly sensitive to the artistic currents of his time.

Those currents, and the ways in which Rilke's reaction to them helps illuminate both his development and his achievement, constitute my emphasis here. Rilke's first, and in some ways lasting, self-conception as a poet involved the views of the French symbolists, views that spread across the world in the last years of the nineteenth century and left their mark on all the arts. The poet, according to this ardent championing of art's mission, was a sort of secular priest, someone who longed for transcendence, rejecting the materialism and pettiness of the world around him (late nineteenth-century culture in Europe, grown opulent on colonialism and unchecked greed, afforded plenty of examples) and seeking escape from a compromised world through a spiritual affirmation of the artistic imagination.

A high calling this, to be a spiritual seeker and voyager, but the exalted conception of art, a rebirth in some ways of the romantic vision, had its dark side. An absence of metaphysical certitude, combined with skepticism about the power of art as a vehicle for any kind of sustained transcendence, meant that the priestly artist was doomed to failure, a decadent figure, a spoiled shaman who could only mix longing with complaint, ardent idealism with rueful acknowledgment of collapse. Oscar Wilde's is one life and career that, especially in the popular imagination, enacts this *fin de siecle* arc of inevitable catastrophe and deterioration. All art was compromised in this view of its combined exaltation and eventual fall, but for artists who dealt in language, most of all poets, there were, additionally and especially, language's own shortcomings, its relativities and dislocations. These could be thought to typify, even to cause, the inevitable breakdown of art's ideals.

To become a modern poet, at least for Rilke's generation, meant finding a way to modify this program, to resolve its dilemmas as an alternative to falling silent (Rimbaud) or succumbing to anomie and entropy (Baudelaire, Mallarmé). Rilke's own answer was twofold. Without abandoning his exalted sense of calling, the dedication that filled his life and took him away from many normal human contacts, he renewed his sense of the artist as craftsman and laborer, sustained by a tradition stretching back through the middle ages and into the classical world. The artist and poet were priests, perhaps, but they were workers too, who had to use their hands, put in long hours, and exhaust themselves with physical effort.

At the same time Rilke helped initiate a relocation of poetry's subject matter, away from a symbolist preoccupation with the occult and with a yearning for transcendence and toward a profound celebration of this world, this life, the particulars that fill our senses and make up our daily existence. Later poets like William Carlos Williams would go much further in this new direction, but they could manage that because the way had been shown by poets like Rilke, who had hammered out an artistic credo and laid a foundation upon which they could build.

To modify the conception of the artist's life, discarding the failed and aborted patterns exemplified by various symbolist prototypes, and also perhaps to bypass the problem of language as a problematic artistic medium, Rilke turned for his role models to the visual arts, to sculpture and painting, and to living and recent exemplars of hard work and imaginative achievement, especially the sculptor Rodin and the painter Cézanne. He more or less apprenticed himself to the former, by becoming his secretary for a time, and his letters about the latter reveal a study of artistic activity and subject matter that the poet would be able to take to heart and modify into a program of his own:

> today I wanted to tell you a little bit about Cézanne. With regard to his work habits, he claimed to have lived as a Bohemian until his fortieth year. Only then, through his acquaintance with Pissarro, did he develop a taste for work. But then to such an extent that for the next thirty years he did nothing *but* work. . . . To achieve the con-

viction and substantiality of things, a reality intensified and potentiated to the point of indestructibility by his experience of the object, seemed to him to be the purpose of his innermost work.

This notion of the artist as one who is totally caught up in hard work, ignoring theory and submerged in practice, helped immensely in offsetting the symbolist prototype of the poet as effete, languid and immobilized by self-pity and excessive self-consciousness, Mallarmé's swan half-frozen in the ice or the suicidal hero ("as for living, our servants can do that for us") of Leconte de Lisle after whom Edmund Wilson named his study of the symbolists, *Axel's Castle*. Rilke could see first-hand how hard and dedicated was Rodin's working life, and he collected anecdotes about the obsessive ways of painters like Van Gogh and Cézanne. It fascinated him too that both these painters appropriated ordinary people and things for their fierce artistic attention:

> . . . he uses his old drawings as models. And lays his apples on bed-covers which Madame Bremond will surely miss some day, and places a wine-bottle among them or whatever happens to be handy. And (like Van Gogh) he makes his 'saints' out of such things; and forces them — *forces them* — to be beautiful, to stand for the whole world and all joy and all glory, and doesn't know whether he has succeeded in making them do it for him.

Here, along with the admiring portrayal of the artist's dogged and obsessive work habits, the way he has of being completely and even a bit comically absorbed in his work, is that shift of attention to the mundane and ordinary that would help Rilke redefine not only the artist but the focus of the art. He made saints too, from the marginalized and despised gallery of figures that make up the "Nine Voices" sequence, to the boldly intimate studies of plants, animals and places that fill the *New Poems* and the *Sonnets to Orpheus*.

10

Rilke never completely turns his back on metaphysics or the symbolist drive toward transcendence, though; he is still, after all, using angels as a primary motif in the late *Duino Elegies*. But the real point of the angels is to repudiate the escapism of transcendence and to bring the divine and the earthly back together, a human engineering of divine incarnation. And Rilke's studies of animals and people and flowers and art objects reflect a program of steady, objective and enormously patient scrutiny that Rodin had urged him to, sending him to the zoo and the Paris parks and museums to single out some object of attention — a panther, a carousel, a statue of Apollo — and study it until it yielded up its fullest meaning and being to him. Two of the flower "still lives" in this collection, the sonnet "Blue Hydrangeas" and the longer, astonishing "The Bowl of Roses" exemplify the poet's growing ability to move sympathetically and completely into his subjects after the manner of painters like Van Gogh and Cézanne, but the same impulse informs his study of human disabilities in the Nine Voices sequence, his re-imagining of myth in "Orpheus. Eurydice. Hermes," and his handling of subjects like the unicorn and the antique fountain in the Orpheus sonnets. A reader feels, in such poems, that the problem of language as rhetoric, as subjectification and falsification of reality, is surmounted and made irrelevant by the psychological and spiritual validity produced from the sympathetic, empathetic, union with the object. We may say that that is not literally possible — the poet must use words and syntax, after all, to achieve his portraiture of being and of what Hopkins called inscape, and the poet cannot escape the limitations of selfhood and historical context — but the response of reader after reader accumulates to a powerful testimony that Rilke did indeed achieve something unique and lasting in these poems, a self-transcendence and a renewal of artistic purpose in the midst of turn-of-the-century decadence. We can go to these poems to be reminded that there may indeed be an independence and power for art that give it a meaningful role in the modern world, a new location for spiritual transmutation. Mapping these complicated exchanges that involve the poet, the subject and the reader, along with a persistent experimentation toward the most expressive possibilities of language, is something that criticism and critical theory have yet to accomplish.

When we have said that Rilke helped reconceive the poet's vocation as a more down-to-earth absorption in craft and have noted the studious objectivity he increasingly brought to the things of this world, we must zig or zag once more, to note that he was, always and at every point in his career, a poet drawn to, and capable of expressing, the ineffable and the mysterious. His credo argued that life is only meaningful when it remains fully open to death, and his capability, as a writer, is always distinctive in part because of his sense of what lies beyond expression, beyond our senses, beyond life itself. If he brings us to a renewed appreciation of a myth, it is apt to be one like the story of Orpheus and Eurydice, where we visit the realm of death. If he trains his attention on an ancient statue, an Apollo or a Buddha, he makes it explode with cosmic meaning. His utmost delight is to mix the earthly and the otherworldly inextricably together, creating a simultaneity that resonates with mystery and excitement, as in his celebration of the Roman sarcophagi in the *Sonnets to Orpheus*, where the old graves he saw around Avignon, empty and having nothing but stillness and nettles to offer, suddenly release "a swarm of elated butterflies," an event that is at once ordinary and magical. This is a poet who can advise with confidence:

> Here in the kingdom of decay, among what's wasting,
> be a tingling glass that shatters itself with sound.
> *(Sonnets to Orpheus*, II, 13)

The confident handling of life and death, change and changelessness, the fearless approach to forbidden topics and closed subjects: this, for many readers, is what makes Rilke not only a personal favorite but a kind of guide to the labyrinth and the underworld, to the mysteries of our mortality and our decisions about how to react to it.

Rilke's life, as he pursued this artistic program, took him on two visits to Russia, in the company of Lou Andreas-Salomé, his first love, who seems to have combined the roles of mentor, mistress and therapist. He was later drawn into the circle of artists at Worpswede, an artist's colony in Germany. There he met and married the sculptor Clara Westhoff and, through his contact with visual artists, began to formulate his modernism. The most gifted artist in the Worpswede group turned out to be his and Clara's close friend, Paula Modersohn-Becker. It was her untimely death after childbirth in 1907, just as she was herself transforming into a leading modernist painter, that led Rilke to write the intricate and moving "Requiem for a Friend," the third section of this selection. Worpswede was finally too provincial for Clara, Paula and Rainer, and the road to greater exposure to what was happening to the arts in the new century led, for all of them at various times, to Paris. There Rilke began his key association with Rodin and his fascination with Cézanne took the form I have described. He also found himself able to visit various attractive European locales, such as Capri, Provence, Rome and Castle Duino on the Adriatic, where aristocratic patronesses helped provide the leisure and solitude he required. Germany and Austria became steadily less attractive, but the poet found himself having to return for the duration of World War One, an experience that silenced him artistically for nearly a decade. France was not the same for him, or for any German-speaking person, after the war. He found a "neutral" territory, finally, in Switzerland, where he settled at Muzot and eventually, in 1922, relocated his inspiration, completing the great *Duino Elegies* and writing the remarkable *Sonnets to Orpheus* in an unprecedented burst of activity. He was already experiencing the first symptoms of the leukemia which would kill him in 1926. His sense that "artistic work and normal living are ultimately an either-or proposition" persisted to the end, although his increasing ability to value and celebrate "normal living" helps articulate the growth of his modernism and his artistic independence from his early models. His simple gravestone at Muzot contains the epitaph he himself composed and which can be translated roughly:

> Rose, oh pure contradiction,
> delighted at being nobody's sleep
> under so many lids.

It is interesting that the epitaph should refer not to the poet and his achievement, but simply be one more attempt to capture the essence of an artistic subject, with rose petals as so many eyelids closing around a paradoxical sleep that is no sleep at all: the inferential relation between the buried poet and the rose is there for us to consider, but this last gesture, like so many of the best ones this poet had made before, is outward, in sympathy and negative capability, toward a simple object of his attentive scrutiny.

In making this selection from Rilke's work I have tried to include poems that I myself have used to introduce students and friends to what I take to be the essence of his achievement. The result is a mixture of his most familiar pieces, the "greatest hits" that one is apt to encounter in anthologies and other attempts at a selective representation, and some less well-known examples that are personal discoveries and favorites suggested by other Rilke enthusiasts. I have found myself drawing on three main sources: *The Book of Pictures*, the first poems of Rilke's real maturity; the *New Poems*, that two-volume collection that is still, for many readers, his most significant and characteristic achievement; and the *Sonnets to Orpheus*, the extraordinary sonnet sequence from the postwar years.

The other major accomplishment (aside from prose work, that is), the 1923 *Duino Elegies,* does not seem to me to excerpt well. My translation of it is still available (from W. W. Norton) and the poem is too much of a piece, I feel, to represent in a volume like this.

The question of whether or not to include the German texts has been a particularly vexing one. Personally, I like readers to be able to visit the translated text and the original indiscriminately and frequently, and would urge that as a practice with this poet and any other. House style for this particular series, along with considerations of cost and space, however, dictated that the book would be English only. I console myself with the knowledge that the German texts of Rilke are easy to come by, sometimes most readily in other volumes that feature a selection of his work: Bly, Mitchell, Herter Norton (not currently in print, alas), Arndt (Rilke's funniest translator, though the humor is generally inadvertent), MacIntyre, Leishman, the two volumes of Edward Snow's complete rendition of the *New Poems* and even, in the case of the Orpheus Sonnets, my complete translation of that work, published by Wesleyan.

Wait, you say: There are all these English versions of Rilke, most of them available and in print, and yet you press forward with one more volume to add to the pile? All I can say by way of self-defense is that this was not done lightly. Many years of reading and teaching Rilke had led me to dissatisfactions, sometimes slight, sometimes acute, with other versions; at the same time, I felt grateful that there were so many Rilkes around in English because comparing and judging them almost always increased my insight into the poem. My friendly "quarrels" with Bly, Mitchell, Herter Norton and others, were productive, and the more numerous the versions of a particular poem, the more I learned. In that spirit, I don't see any harm in contributing another selection to the available stock of Rilke in English, and would hope that even

readers who are mostly intent on hunting down my short-
comings as a translator will find themselves thereby closer
to a good understanding of Rilke. He deserves it.

NOTES

The citations from Rilke's letters are from *Letters on Cézanne*,
translated by Joel Agee, Fromm International, New York, 1985,
pp. 34 and 40.

I wish especially to acknowledge the help of Stuart Friebert,
who carefully compared my versions to the German and helped
me be more accurate and more resourceful as a translator. His
insights into Rilke's poetry and language were indispensable.

The selections from *Sonnets to Orpheus* are reprinted with the
permission of Wesleyan University Press and the University Press
of New England.

I

from *The Book of Pictures*

ENTRANCE

Whoever you are: go out at evening,
leaving your room, where everything's familiar;
between you and the distance lies your house:
whoever you are.
With tired eyes, that scarcely pull themselves
up and away from the worn-down threshold,
you slowly lift up one black tree
and place it against the sky: slim, alone.
And you have made the world. And it is large
and like a word that's ripening in silence.
And as your will takes in the sense of it,
your eyes can gently let it go . . .

THE ANGELS

All of them have weary mouths
and bright souls without a seam.
And a longing (as toward sin)
goes sometimes through their dream.

Each is like all the others;
hushed in God's garden, silently,
like many, many intervals
in His might and melody.

Only when they spread their wings
are they the wakers of a wind:
As if with His wide sculptor-hands
God was turning pages
in the dark book of first beginnings.

CHILDHOOD

School time runs on and on with anxiousness
and boredom, full of pauses, full of pointless things.
Oh solitude, oh slow and heavy hours. . .
And then outside: the streets glisten and ring
and in the squares the fountains play
and in the gardens all the world grows huge. —
And one runs through it all in a small suit
quite differently than others go, or went —:
Oh wonderful, odd moments, oh heavy hours,
oh solitude.

And looking out so far and seeing things:
men and women, men, men, women,
and children who are different, brightly dressed,
and there a house, and now and then a dog
and fear that can turn quietly to trust —:
oh sadness with no sense, oh dream, oh horror,
oh bottomless abyss.

And so to play: ball and top and hoop
in gardens that are softly losing color,
and sometimes to brush past adults,
blind and unruly from a game of tag,
but quieted by nightfall, walking home
with stiff little steps, held firmly by the hand —:
Oh always more elusive comprehension,
oh fear, oh heavy weight.

And hours at a time by the big gray pond,
kneeling with a little sailboat there;
and to forget it because those other sails
more interesting than yours are cutting circles,
and then to have to think about the small white

face that sank away and shone out from the pond:
oh childhood, oh disappearing images,
where to? where to?

FROM A CHILDHOOD

The darkening was like treasure in the room
where the boy sat, withdrawn and secretive.
And when, as in a dream, his mother entered,
a glass quivered in the silent sideboard.
She felt the room had given her away
and kissed her boy: you're here? . . .
Then both looked anxiously at the piano,
for often, evenings, she would sing a song
in which the boy was strangely, deeply caught.

He sat stock still. His big look hung
right on her hand, bowed down by its ring,
moving across white keys as if
it made its way through heavy snowdrifts.

PEOPLE BY NIGHT

Nights are not made for crowds.
Night sets you apart from your neighbor
and you shall not seek him in spite of it.
And if you light your room at night
to look people in the face,
then you must consider: whose?

People are frightening in the light
that drips from their faces,
and if they've assembled at night
you stare at a wavering world
all run together on itself.
The yellow that shines on their foreheads
has banished all of their thoughts,
wine flares in their gazes,
the gestures with which they converse
hang like weights on their hands;
and what they are saying is: I and I,
meaning: anyone.

EVENING

The evening gradually puts on the clothes
held for it by an ancient row of trees;
you watch, and now your world takes leave of you,
with one part going toward heaven and one that falls;

they leave you not belonging much to either,
not quite so dark as the now silent house,
not quite so ready to call on the eternal
as that which turns to star each night and rises;

they leave you speechless, trying to unsnarl
your life that's frightened, huge and ripening,
that turns, partly confused, partly enlightened,
sometimes to stone in you, sometimes to star.

LONELINESS

Loneliness is like a rain.
It rises from the sea to meet the evenings;
from plains that stretch into the distance
it goes up to the sky, that always has it.
From the sky it falls upon the town.

It rains down in those mongrel hours
when all the streets are turning toward the day,
and when those bodies that got nothing from each other
go separate ways, sad and disappointed;
when people who feel hate for one another
must sleep together in one bed;

then loneliness goes down into the rivers . . .

FALL DAY

Lord: it's time. Summer was very large.
Lay your shadow on the sundials now
and let the winds loose in the meadows.

Tell the last fruits they must be full;
give them two more perfect southern days,
force them to completion and then chase
their last sweetness into the heavy wine.

Who has no house now won't be building one.
Who is alone will stay that way for long,
will waken, read, write lengthy letters
and wander, restless, up and down
the avenues when leaves are blowing.

The Voices: Nine Poems with a Titlepage

TITLEPAGE

The rich and happy are right to keep silent,
nobody wants to know what they're like.
But unfortunates have to exhibit themselves,
have to say: I'm blind,
or: I'm about to become that way,
or: things aren't too good for me here on earth,
or: I have a sick child,
or: here's where I'm held together . . .

And perhaps even that doesn't do it.

And since everyone goes past them
the way they go past things,
sometimes they have to sing.

And then you can hear some good singing.

People are really strange; they'd rather
hear castrati in boys' choirs.

But God comes, in person, and stays a long time
when these eunuchs manage to rouse him.

THE BEGGAR'S SONG

I always go from door to door,
rain-drenched or burned by sun;
All of a sudden I cup my right ear
in my right hand.
Then my own voice seems to me
as if I've never known it.

Then I don't know for sure who's screaming,
me or somebody else.
I cry for a pittance.
The poets cry for more.

And I'm finally able to shut my face
by shutting both my eyes;
as it lies in my hand with its weight,
it looks like rest itself.
So people won't think I don't have a place
where I can lay my head.

THE BLIND MAN'S SONG

I'm blind, you out there, that's a curse,
a disgust, a contradiction,
something heavy every day.
I put my hand on my wife's arm,
my gray hand on her gray gray,
and she leads me through nothing but emptiness.

You move and stir and think your sound
is different from stone on stone,
but you're wrong: I alone
live and suffer and yell.
There's an endless cry inside me,
and I don't even know if it comes
from my heart or from my bowels.

Are my songs familiar? You never sang them,
not with these intonations.
The new light comes to you each morning
warm in your open apartment.
And you have that feeling of face to face
that tempts you into mercy.

THE DRINKER'S SONG

It wasn't in me. It went out and in.
I wanted to hold it. The wine held it instead.
(I don't even know what it was anymore.)
Then it held out that and this to me
until I belonged to it totally.
Such a fool.

Now I'm a part of its game, and it deals
me out, sneering, and maybe today it'll
lose me to that beast, Death.
When he's won me, grubby old card,
he'll use me to scratch his gray scabs
then toss me away in the mud.

THE SUICIDE'S SONG

So then, one more moment. . .
They keep on finding ways to cut
my rope. This last time,
I really was ready, and I
already had some eternity
down in my gut.

They thrust the spoon toward me,
this spoon of life.
No, I don't and I won't even sip,
just let me throw up.

I know that the world's a brimming
pot, I know life's ready and good,
but it doesn't go into my blood,
it just goes right to my head.

Others it nourishes, me it makes sick;
see, I have to deny it.
For a thousand years or so
I'm going to need to diet.

THE WIDOW'S SONG

In the beginning my life was good.
It kept me warm, it made me strong.
That it does that to all the young —
how could I see that then?
I didn't know what life was like —,
all at once it was just year upon year,
no longer good, no longer new, no longer wonderful,
as if it had ripped in half.

That wasn't his fault and it wasn't mine;
we both had patience to spare,
but Death has none at all.
I saw him coming (how vile he was),
and I watched as he took and took;
it wasn't mine after all.

Then what was mine; mine alone, mine?
Wasn't my misery, even,
something on loan from fate?
Fate doesn't just want the happiness back,
it claims the pain and the crying too,
and it buys up disaster, second-hand.

Fate was right there, and paid almost nothing
for every expression on my face,
right down to the way I walk.
Every day was a fire sale,
and when I was empty, it abandoned me
and left me standing open.

THE IDIOT'S SONG

They let me go, they don't get in my way.
They say, he'll be okay.
How nice.
Nothing can happen. All things come and coast
around and around the Holy Ghost,
around that particular Ghost (you know) —,
how nice.

No, don't think there's any danger, there's
no danger here at all.
There is the blood, of course.
Blood is the heaviest. Blood's very heavy,
sometimes I think I can't take any more —.
(How nice.)

Oh, look at that beautiful ball;
red and round like an Everywhere.
Nice that you created it.
Do you think it will come when I call?

How strangely everything acts,
streaming together, swimming apart:
friendly, a little hard to make out;
how nice.

THE ORPHAN'S SONG

I'm nobody and I never will be somebody.
Too small to exist right now
and in the future too.

Mothers and fathers,
pity me!

I'm not worth the trouble of raising:
I'll be mowed down, that's my fate.
I can't be useful: now it's too early,
tomorrow it's too late.

I just have this one little dress,
it's getting worn and faded,
it has to last an eternity
if I should come before God.

I just have this lock of hair
(it always stays the same, somehow),
somebody's dearest possession once.

He doesn't love anything now.

THE DWARF'S SONG

Maybe my soul is straight and good;
but my heart, my twisted blood,
everything else that makes me hurt,
is more than it can heft.
It has no garden, it has no bed,
it hangs on my sharp skeleton,
beating its terrified wings.

From my hands too — don't expect more.
Look how stubby they are:
they flop and hop, heavy and damp,
like little toads after rain.
Everything else about me
is shabby and old and sad;
why does God even hesitate
to throw it all out on the dungheap?

Is he angry about my face
with its mean and twisted mouth?
Often it wanted to turn
all bright and clear, right through;
but nobody came up as close to it
as the great big dogs do.
And dogs don't have what I want.

THE LEPER'S SONG

Look, I'm the one they've all disowned.
Because of my leprosy,
no one in town has to know me.
And I shake my rattle,
knocking my sorry appearance
into everybody's ear
that happens to come near.
And those who hear its wooden sound,
don't even look around,
and what has happened here,
they don't want to know any more.

Within my rattle's range,
I'm quite at home; but maybe
you're making my rattle so loud
that people who won't come near
don't even want to be far.
Which means I can go a long way
and never come upon anyone — girl,
woman or man or child. . .

Animals I wouldn't want to scare.

II

from *New Poems*

LOVESONG

How shall I manage my soul so that it
doesn't touch against yours? How shall I
lift it past you to get to other things?
Oh, I would gladly shelter it
in darkness, near something lost,
in a strange and silent place
that doesn't hum and resound
each time your depths vibrate.
But everything that touches you or me
takes us together, as a violin bow
strokes one sound from two adjoining strings.
What kind of instrument are we stretched out on?
And what musician holds us in his grasp?
O sweet song.

THE PANTHER

His gaze, from passing all those bars,
is too tired for anything more.
It seems to him there are a thousand bars
and past those thousand bars no world.

The soft gait of supple flex and power
that pads around the smallest circle here
is like a dance of strength around a point
in which a mighty will stands dazed.

Once in a while the curtain of the pupil
parts silently—. An image goes in then,
runs through the trembling stillness of the limbs
and vanishes inside the heart.

SAINT SEBASTIAN

He stands like someone lying down,
propped up by his own huge will.
Off somewhere else, like mothers when they nurse,
and bound in himself like a wreath.

And the arrows arrive: now, and now,
as if they sprang out of his thighs,
iron and trembling at the ends. And still
he smiles darkly, he's not hurt.

Just once a sadness suddenly looms large,
and his eyes grow naked with pain
until they deny something, not worth the trouble,
filling with scorn as they come to relinquish
those who would kill a beautiful thing.

THE ANGEL

With the slightest of nods he dismisses
all bonds and duties, whatever's constricting;
for his own heart's tuned, through its steady pulses,
to the great circles of eternal coming.

The deep skies lie before him, full of shapes,
and each can call to him: come to me, know me —.
Don't ask his empty hands to carry
the things that weigh you down. Just this:

that they come to you at night, to test you,
and go through the house like someone rage has filled,
and grab you as if they were going to create you
and break you right out of your mold.

THE SWAN

This straining to get through all that's undone,
this hardship and this sense of being bound,
are like the awkward walking of the swan.

And dying, when we loosen our tight hold
of the firm earth on which we daily stand,
is like the flustered way the swan lets down

into the water, current that receives
him easily, then happily runs back
beneath him, wave on easy wave,
while he, now wholly still and sure,
more royal, stately and mature,
calmly allows it to carry him on.

DEATH-EXPERIENCE

We don't know anything about this passing on — it
never shares with us. We have no basis
for showing admiration, love or hate
to Death, whose mouth the mask of tragic

lamentation disfigures so grotesquely.
The world remains full of the roles we play.
And as long as we try to please and get applause
Death plays along as well, although he doesn't please.

But when you left, our stage was suddenly
lit by a flash — reality broke through
the crack you left by: green that was really green,
real sunlight, a forest that was real.

We go on acting. Fearful, speaking lines
that we had trouble learning, lifting hands
in the set gestures; but your existence,
vanished from us and from our play,

will sometimes come across us as
a thought of that reality sinks in,
and for a while then, carried away,
we play life true, not thinking of applause.

BLUE HYDRANGEAS

These leaves are like the last vestige of green
you find in dye-pots, rough and dull and dry,
behind some blossom-clusters wearing blue
that's not their own, mirrored from far away.

They mirror it vaguely and tearfully,
as if they secretly wished it gone again;
and just like old blue stationery, they
have yellow tints, and violets and grays;

as faded as a much-washed child's apron
no longer used, with nothing else to happen:
you feel how short the little life has been.

Then all at once the blue seems to renew
in one of the clusters, and you see how
a touching blue delights itself in green.

PORTRAIT OF MY FATHER IN HIS YOUTH

Dream in the eyes. The forehead seems to be
in touch with something distant. A huge amount
of youth around the mouth and a seductiveness
that hasn't learned to smile. Held before
the ornamental lacings of the slim
aristocratic uniform: the saber's basket-hilt
and both the hands — they wait there
peacefully, they reach for nothing.
By now they're scarcely visible, as though
they need, those graspers of the far, to be
the first to disappear. And all the rest
is curtained off, erased, as though
no one could fathom it, cloudy from its depths —.

You swiftly fading photograph
in my more slowly fading hands.

THE CAROUSEL

Jardin du Luxembourg

With a roof and its shadow, for a little spell,
it turns its herd of piebald horses round,
beasts from that country that holds on so long
before it goes under for good.
Sure, some are hitched to wagons, but
it's clear they still have spirit;
a bad red lion goes around with them,
and now and then a snow-white elephant.

There's even a bear, just like in the forest,
except that he's wearing a saddle
with a little blue girl strapped on.

And on the lion rides a boy in white,
holding on with his small, hot fist,
while the lion snarls and lolls his tongue.

And now and then a snow-white elephant.

And on the horses, coming by,
bright girls who have almost outgrown
this horseplay; in mid-ride
they gaze out somewhere else, in this direction.

And now and then a snow-white elephant.

All this goes hurrying towards its end,
circling and twirling aimlessly.
A red, a green, a gray go sailing past,
and a little profile, scarcely formed.
And sometimes a smile, turned this way,
blissful, that dazzles and then vanishes
once more into the blind and breathless game.

SPANISH DANCER

The way a kitchen match, held in your hand,
glows white before it turns to flame and throws
small twitching tongues to every side —: within
the ring of eager watchers, hot and bright,
her round dance starts to twitch and spread itself.

And suddenly it is completely flame.

With one quick glance she sets her hair on fire
and then goes on with risky art to whirl
her whole dress round within this roaring blaze
from which her naked arms, like startled snakes,
stretch up and out, aroused and rattling.

And then: as if she felt the fire get tight,
she gathers it in front and throws it down
quite scornfully, with a commanding gesture,
and sees it lying there upon the ground
raging and flaming, refusing to give in —.
But she, in charge of it and with a sweet
welcoming smile, looks up at us exuberantly
and stamps it out with strong and tiny feet.

ORPHEUS. EURYDICE. HERMES

This was the fabulous mine of souls.
Like silver ore they went,
veins in its hushed dark. Between roots
the blood welled up that goes toward human beings,
looking as hard as porphyry in that dark.
Nothing else was red.

Rocky cliffs were there
and shadow forests. Bridges across emptiness
and that one gray and blind pond
that hung above its distant bed
like a rainy sky above a landscape.
And between the meadows, soft and full of patience,
the one path's pale stripe showed itself,
like a long pallor, stretching on.

And up this path they came.

In front the slender man in the blue cloak,
mute and impatient, staring straight ahead.
His strides ate up the path in giant bites,
that never paused to chew; his hands hung down
heavy and clenched below the falling folds,
no longer aware of the weightless lyre
that had grown right into his left hand
like rose-stems grown into an olive branch.
And his senses felt as though they'd split in two:
his sight would bound before him like a dog,
turn round, come back, then race away again
and wait, standing, at the path's next bend, —
but his hearing, like an odor, hung behind.
Sometimes he thought that it had reached
to the footsteps of the other two

who were to follow him on this long climb.
And then it seemed as if his own steps' echo
and the breeze stirred up by his cloak
were all that was behind him.
But he told himself they were still coming;
said it out loud, heard it die away.
They were still coming, it was just that both
walked so very lightly. If he could
just once turn round (if his looking back
were not the ruin of this enterprise,
still incomplete), then he'd *have* to see them,
these two light walkers following him so silently:

The god of wayfaring and distant tidings,
a traveler's hood above his shining eyes,
the slender staff held out before his body,
the wings beating at his ankles;
and holding on to his left hand: *she*.

The one so loved that from one lyre
more lamentation rose than from
lamenting women: lament
that made itself into a world of woe, in which
all things were re-created: wood and dale
and path and village, field and stream and beast;
until around this lamentation-world, just as
around the other earth, a sun
and a silent, star-filled heaven moved,
a lamentation-heaven with distorted stars —:
this woman, loved so much.

But now she walked along beside that god,
her steps encumbered by long winding-sheets,
confused, gentle, and without impatience.
She was absorbed, like a woman great with hope,
and took no notice of the man who walked ahead
or of the path that led them up toward life.

54

She was absorbed. And her death-existence
filled her like fullness itself.
Like a fruit ripe with sweetness and darkness,
she was that full of her big death
and it was still so new to her
that she could take in nothing.

She was inside a new virginity
and was untouchable; her sex was closed
like a young flower in the evening,
and her hands had now grown so unused to marriage
that even the light god's guiding touch,
endlessly gentle, sickened her,
like too much intimacy.

She was no longer that blond woman
who sometimes echoed in the poet's songs,
no longer the wide bed's fragrance and island,
and that man's property no more.

She was already loosened like long hair,
and given away like fallen rain,
and shared like provisions a hundred times over.

She was already root.

And when, all at once,
the god stopped her and with pain in his voice
spoke the words: He has turned around —,
she understood nothing and said softly: *Who*?

But far off, darkly outlined at the shining gate,
someone or other stood, whose countenance
could hardly be made out. He stood and saw
how on that strip of meadow path
with a sad glance the god of tidings
turned silently around, following that shape

that was already going back along the path,
steps encumbered by long winding sheets,
confused, gentle, and without impatience.

THE BOWL OF ROSES

Angry ones: you saw them flare up, saw two boys
ball themselves into a something
that was all hatred, tumbling on the ground
like an animal attacked by bees;
actors, towering overstaters,
raging horses, crashing to collapse,
eyes rolling, baring their teeth
as if the skull was going to peel itself,
starting from the mouth.

But now you know how that's forgotten:
this full bowl of roses stands before you,
unforgettable, filled to the brim
with the utmost expression of being, bending,
yielding, unable to give, simply existing,
that could ever be ours: utmost for us too.

Silent life, opening and opening, no end in sight,
a use of space that takes no space away
from space that things around it need,
an existence with almost no outlines, all background
and pure inwardness, and much strange softness
and self-illuminated — right to the rim:
do we know anything, anywhere, that's like this?

Then like this: that emotion is born
from the touch of petal to petal?
And this: that a petal comes open like an eyelid
and underneath are just more eyelids, nothing else,
closed, as though they had to be asleep
ten times deeper to shut down visionary power.
And this above all: that through these petals
light somehow has to pass. From a thousand bright skies

they slowly filter each drop of darkness
within whose fiery luster the tangled group
of stamens stirs and rears erect.

And the movement in the roses — look:
gestures from such small angles of eruption
they'd never be noticed if not for the way
their rays fan out to the cosmos.

Look at that white one; it has opened in bliss
and stands there in its great splayed petals
like a Venus erect in her shell;
and the blushing one, that turns and leans
as if embarrassed, toward the one that's cool,
and how that cool one won't respond, withdraws,

and how a cold one stands, wrapped in itself,
among the opening ones, that shed everything.
And *what* they shed: how it is light or heavy,
how it can be a cloak, a load, a wing
and then a mask, now this, now that,
and *how* they shed it: as if before a lover.

Is there anything they can't become? Wasn't
that yellow one, lying there hollow and open,
the rind of a fruit where the very same color,
more concentrated, orangey-red, was juice?
And was unfurling just too much for this one,
because in the air its anonymous pink
has picked up a bitter aftertaste of violet?
And the one made of cambric, isn't it a dress
to which the soft and breath-warm slip still clings,
both of them tossed aside in morning shadows
near an old pool in the forest?
And this one, opalescent porcelain,
easily shattered, a shallow china cup

filled with small, lit butterflies, —
and that one, which holds nothing but itself.

Aren't all of us like that, containing just ourselves,
if self-containment means: transforming the outside
        world
and wind and rain and spring's great patience
and guilt and restlessness and masquerading fate
and the darkening of the earth at evening
and even the clouds that change and flow and vanish,
and even the vague command of the distant stars
all changed to a handful of inwardness.

It now lies carefree in these open roses.

ARCHAIC TORSO OF APOLLO

We've never known the legendary head
where the eye-apples ripened. But
his torso glows still, like a candelabrum
in which his gaze, turned down,

contains itself and shines. Otherwise
the breast-curve wouldn't blind you so, nor would
the hips and groin form toward that smile
whose center held the seeds of procreation.

And then this stone would stand here, short and broken,
under the shoulders' clear, cascading plunge
and wouldn't ripple like a wild beast's fur

and break with light from every surface
like a star: because there is no place
that doesn't see you. You must change your life.

FADING

Lightly, as though after death,
she wears her gloves and her shawl.
A scent from her bureau drawers
has replaced the enjoyable smell

by which she once knew herself.
She no longer asks now, who
she might be (:a distant relation),
but goes around abstractedly

and cares for an apprehensive room,
making it neat and secure,
because perhaps it's still
the very same girl living there.

VENICE IN LATE AUTUMN

The city now no longer drifts like bait
to catch the newly rising days.
Against your glance the glassy palaces
feel still more brittle, pinging. And summer hangs

from every garden like a heap of puppets,
heads lolling, tired, all used up.
But from old forest-skeletons, down deep,
determination rises: as though overnight

the Admiral of the Seas could double
the galleys in his wakeful arsenal,
tarring the morning breeze with his great fleet

which pushes out with all oars beating
and then, flags rising and unfurling,
takes the great wind, shining and charged with fate.

THE FLAMINGOS

Jardin des Plantes, Paris

In mirror-pictures, as by Fragonard,
no more conception of their white and red
is given than if someone offered
to tell you of his mistress and then said:

she was still soft with sleep. Rising in green,
swaying on rosy stilts, blooming together,
they stand like flowers in a border,
seducing more seductively than Phryne,

but just themselves; necks snaking down,
they bury their pale eyes among their own
softness that conceals both black and apple-red.

A scream of envy shakes the aviary;
but they have stretched out in amazement
and stride alone into imagined worlds.

BUDDHA IN GLORY

Center of all centers, core of cores,
almond, closed round itself and growing sweet —
everything here and out to all the stars
is your own fruit-flesh: it's you we greet.

See, you feel now how things no longer cling;
your rind is out there in infinity,
there where the strong juice gathers, brims.
And from beyond, a radiance helps bring

ripeness as all your countless suns
turn in their courses, glowing and full.
While inside you, already, something's begun
that will outlast them all.

III

**Requiem for a Friend
(1908)**

REQUIEM FOR A FRIEND

I have some dead, and I have let them go
and been surprised to see them so good-natured,
making themselves at home in death, so easy,
so different from the reputation. Just you, you come
back; you graze me, haunt me, you try
bumping things that will shiver and ring,
to give you away. Oh, don't take from me what I've
slowly learned! I'm right; you're wrong
if you think you need to feel homesick
for anything that's here. We change these things,
transfigure them; the world isn't here, we mirror it
into our own existence as soon as we perceive it.

I thought you'd made more progress. I'm dismayed
that *you* would get confused, come back, who did
more transfiguring than any other woman.
That we were terrified by your death — no, that
your hard death interrupted us, darkly,
tearing the time beforehand from the aftermath:
that's our concern; putting that back together
will be our job. But that
you too were terrified, that you're even having
some terror now, there where terror has no meaning;
that you'd give up any piece of your eternity
and come back here, my dear friend, here,
where everything's still not come to life;
or that out there, where everything's infinite,
    overwhelmed
and inattentive in your first encounter,
you somehow didn't grasp the greatness of it all
the way you grasped each single thing on earth;
that from the orbit you'd already entered

the mute force of some old upset
should drag you back into our counted time —:
this often wakes me up at night
like a burglar, breaking in.

If I could say you've only come
peacefully, out of kindness, generous abundance,
because you are so sure, so self-possessed,
that you can scoot around anywhere, like a child,
with no fear of places where anyone can do
bad things to you — but no: you're *asking* something.
That goes right down into my bones, cuts like a saw.
An accusation, as if carried by your ghost,
pursuing me when I withdraw at night
into my lungs, into my bowels,
into the last poor chamber of my heart, —
that wouldn't be as bad as this dim *asking*.
What is it that you want?

Tell me, am I supposed to travel?
Did you leave behind some object that is suffering,
something that wants to come after you?
Must I go visit some country
you never saw, though it was as close
as the other side of your senses?

I want to travel its rivers, go ashore,
ask about its oldest customs,
stand talking with its women in their doorways
and watch as they call their children home.

I want to notice how they wear
the landscape there, doing the old work
of fields and meadows; to hanker after
being led before their king;
want to charm their priests with bribes

to lay me down before their most important idol
and lock the temple doors . . .

Then when I've learned a lot,
I'll simply watch the animals, till something
in the way they turn and move
enters my own limbs and joints;
I want to have a brief existence in their eyes
that take me up and gently let me go,
relaxed, making no judgments.
I'll have the gardeners name the many flowers for me
so I can bring back proper names in pots,
beautiful remnants of a hundred or more odors.
And I'll buy fruits, fruits that contain
that country still, even its skies!

Because that's what you understood: full fruits.
You used to set them out in bowls before you
and weigh their heaviness with colors.
And you saw those women too as fruits
and the children, just as though from inside out,
expanding into the shapes of their existence.
And finally you saw yourself as fruit,
took yourself out of your clothes; carried
yourself to the mirror, let yourself into it
right up to your gaze, kept the gaze large before it,
and did not say: that's me; no: this *is*.
And so incurious was your gaze at last,
so unacquisitive, so truly vowed to poverty,
it didn't even need you any more: holy.
That's how I want to recall you, the way
you presented yourself, deep inside the mirror,
far from everything else. Why come any other way?
Why deny yourself? Why would you have me think
that in the amber beads you wore around your neck
there was still something heavy, that heaviness

that never exists in the serene beyond of paintings?
Why seem to show me some evil omen by the way you
       stand?
What makes you lay out the contours of your body
like the lines inside a hand, making me see them
only as some outline of your fate?

Come into the candlelight. I'm not afraid
to look the dead in the face. When they return
they have a right to stand there in our gaze
the same as other things.
Come here; and we'll be quiet for a bit.

Look at this rose on my desk:
isn't the light around it just as timid
as the light on you? It shouldn't be here either.
It should have bloomed or withered out there in the
       garden,
without involving me, — now it goes on like this,
and what is my awareness to it?

Don't be afraid if I begin to grasp it now:
oh, it's rising up in me, I have to
grasp its meaning, I'd have no choice,
even if it killed me. I do see why you're here,
I understand exactly. The way
a blind man grasps a nearby object, feeling it all over,
I feel your fate, and know no name for it.

Let us grieve together, that someone
took you right out of your mirror. Can you still cry?
You can't. You turned
the strength and pressure of your tears
into your ripe gazing, and you were changing
all of the juices inside you
into a strong existence that would rise
and circulate, unseeing and in equilibrium.

Then chance stepped in and took you, your last chance,
back from your farthest progress, into a world where
    juices
insist on having things their way.

Not all at once. It didn't tear you fully;
at first it only tore a piece. But then
around this piece, day after day,
reality gathered, making it heavy,
until it took all your attention;
you had to go to it and break in pieces
according to the law, yourself, with effort,
spending your entire self.
And from the night-warm soil of your heart
you grubbed the seeds up, seeds still green,
from which your death would sprout: yours,
your own death to your own life.
And then you ate them, your death-seeds,
as you would any others, ate the seeds
and found an aftertaste of sweetness
you hadn't intended, sweetness on your lips,
you: already so sweet within your senses.

Oh let us grieve. Do you know,
when you called your own blood back
from its incomparable orbit, how unwillingly,
how hesitantly, it returned?
How it resumed life's narrow little cycles,
all confused. How mistrustfully
it entered the placenta, suddenly
all tired out from the long way home?
You drove it on, you pushed it, dragged it
up to the hearth, the way you'd drag
a group of animals towards sacrifice;
and wanted it, despite all, to be happy.
And finally you succeeded: it *was* happy,
and it came forward and gave up. And you thought,

because you had grown used to other measurements,
that this would only be a little while;
but you were back in normal time now,
and normal time is long. And times goes on,
and time expands, and time is like a relapse
into an illness.

How short your life was if you compare it
to those hours when you sat there, bending
the lush forces of your own lush future
down toward the child-seed within you
that was becoming fate. Oh heavy work,
work that surpassed your strength. You did it,
day after day, dragging yourself forward
to pull the lovely weaving from the loom
and use the threads all differently.
And finally you had heart enough to celebrate.

Then, because it was over, you wanted a reward,
just like children when they've had to drink
some bittersweet tea to make them better.
This is the way you rewarded yourself:
because you were too far apart from everyone,
as you still are; nobody could have guessed
what the right treat for you would be.
You knew it. You sat up
in that same bed you'd given birth in
and a mirror stood before you, one that gave
everything right back to you. Now everything was *you*,
and right up front, and anything deeper was just
        deception
the lovely deception of any woman who likes
to put jewelry on and combs her hair and changes.

And then you died as women used to die
in the old days, died in the warm house,
died the old-fashioned death of women lying in,

women who are trying to close themselves
back up again but can't, because the darkness
to which they've also given birth
comes back, pushes its way in, and enters.
Oh shouldn't they have found
some wailing women for you? Women you can pay
to howl the whole night through, when it's too quiet?
Rituals, please! We no longer have enough
rituals. They've all been talked away.
That's why you've had to come back, dead,
and here, with me, review some grieving.
Can you hear me grieving? I'd like to fling my voice
out like a cloth across the remnants of your death
and shred it to pieces until everything I say
goes dressed in rags from that torn voice, goes freezing.
If mourning were enough. But now I must accuse:
not the man who took you from yourself
(I'll never trace him, he's like all of us),
still, I accuse in him: the man.

If somewhere deep within me rises up
a sense of having been a child I still don't know,
maybe the very purest essence of my childhood:
I don't want to know it. Without even looking,
I'll make an angel from it and then hurl it
into the front rank of crying angels, angels who
        remember God.

Because this suffering's gone on too long,
no one can stand it, it's too heavy for us,
this crazy sorrow caused by phony love
that builds on its traditions like a habit,
and calls itself a right, luxuriant from injustice.
Where is one man who has the right of ownership?
Who can possess what cannot hold itself
but just from time to time can catch itself
and, blissful, throw itself again, the way

a child throws a ball? As little as the general can possess
the carved Nike on his vessel's prow
when the mysterious lightness of her godhead
suddenly lifts her into the bright sea wind:
that's how little one can call a woman back
who, seeing us no longer, goes on forward
along some narrow strip of her existence,
miraculously, without a misstep:
unless of course he has a bent for guilt.

For *this* is guilt, if anything is guilt:
not to enlarge the freedom of a love
with all the freedom we would wish ourselves.
We need, where we love, just this:
to let each other go; for holding on
is something we do naturally, it takes no practice.

Are you still there? What corner are you standing in?
You knew so much about all this
and got so much accomplished, going along
open to all things, like a breaking day.
Women suffer: to love is to be alone,
and artists realize sometimes, in their work,
that they must keep transforming, where they love.
You began both; and both exist in what
your fame, detaching them from you,
begins to disfigure now.
Oh, you were well beyond any fame. You were
unobtrusive; you had softly, quietly,
taken your beauty,
the way one takes a flag down
on the gray morning of a working-day,
and wanted nothing but a good long spell of work
that's left unfinished: in spite of everything, not finished.

If you're still there, if in this darkness
there's still a place in which your spirit

quivers and floats on the shallow sound-waves
of one single voice, raised alone at night
in the air that moves in a high-ceilinged room:
hear me; help me. You see, we slide back
not knowing that we're doing it,
back from our own achievement
into ways we don't intend or want, in which
we're trapped, as in a dream,
and where we die, unable to wake up.
No one goes farther. Anyone who has lifted
his blood up high in a long spell of work
can have this happen, he can't keep carrying it
and it falls back from its own weight, worthless.
For somewhere there's an ancient hatred
between our normal life and the great work.
That I may see into it, and say it: help me.

Don't come back. If you can stand it,
stay dead with the dead. The dead are busy.
But help me in a way that doesn't harm you,
the way what's distant sometimes helps the most: inside
    me.

IV

from *Sonnets to Orpheus*

A tree stood up. Oh pure uprising!
Orpheus is singing! Oh tall tree in the ear!
And everything grew still. Yet in the silence there
changes took place, signals and fresh beginnings.

Creatures of stillness crowded from the clear
untangled woods, from nests and lairs;
and it turned out that their light stepping
came not from fear or from cunning

but so they could listen. Shriek, bellow and roar
had shrunk in their hearts. And while before
there was scarcely a hut where they might stay,

just a shelter made of the darkest cravings
with shaky posts for an entrance-way —
you made a temple for them in their hearing.

From the joined happiness of song and lyre
a girl, almost, was formed, came forth, glowed
clearly through her April veils, and made
a bed for herself inside my ear.

And slept in me. And then her sleep was
everything: trees I had wondered at, those
vivid distances, the meadow I felt, every
amazement that had ever been inside me.

She slept the world. Singing god, how did
you make her so whole she didn't first
need to be awake? See, she rose up, still asleep.

Where's her death? Do you have time to find
that subject before your song burns up?
Where does she drain out of me? . . . a girl,
        almost . . .

A god can do it. But tell me how
a man can follow him through the narrow
lyre. The human self is split; where two
heartways cross, there is no temple to Apollo.

Song, as you teach it, is not desire, not
a wooing of something that's finally attained;
song is existence. Easy for the god. But
when do *we* exist? And when does he spend

the earth and the stars on our being?
When we love? That's what you think when you're
        young;
not so, though your voice forces open your mouth, —

learn to forget how you sang. That fades.
Real singing is a different kind of breath.
A nothing-breath. A ripple in the god. A wind.

Don't lay a stone to his memory. The rose
can bloom, if you like, once a year for his sake.
For Orpheus *is* the rose. His metamorphosis
takes this form, that form. No need to think

about his other names. Once and for all:
when there's singing, it's Orpheus. He comes and goes.
It's enough if sometimes he stays several
days; more, say, than a bowl of roses.

He has to vanish so you can understand.
Even if it frightens him to disappear.
While his word is transforming our beings here

he's somewhere else, past following.
The lyre's grill doesn't pinch his hands.
Even as he breaks rules, he's obeying.

Is he of this world? No, he gets
his large nature from both realms. To know
how best to curve the willow's boughs
you have to have been through its roots.

Don't leave bread or milk on the table
at night: that attracts the dead.
But under your own mild eyelids
you can let this conjuror mingle

that sight of the dead into all that you've seen;
and may the magic of earthsmoke and meadow rue
be as true as the clearest relation.

Nothing should spoil good images; whether
they came from a grave or a bedroom,
let him praise finger-ring, buckle, and pitcher.

You've never been away from me, antique
sarcophagi, but I greet you — you
whom jubilant waters have flowed through
since Roman days, as wandering music.

Or those old graves, wide open, like the eyes
of a shepherd who wakes up feeling joyful,
— full of stillness and blossoming nettles —
releasing a swarm of elated butterflies;

all that we snatch away from doubt
I greet, mouths that are open once more,
having learned what silence means.

Have *we* learned that? Or have we yet
to learn? Both. Hesitating between
is what gives our faces character.

Wait . . . that tastes good . . . Already it's leaving.
. . . Just a faint music, a stamping, a humming —:
Girls who are warm, girls who are silent,
dance the taste of this sampled fruit!

Dance the orange. Who can forget how, drowning
in itself, it still resists the tendency
to be too sweet. Yours in possessing
it has turned into you, deliciously.

Dance the orange. Throw its warmer landscape
out of yourselves, let the ripeness shine
in its native air! Peel away, radiant,

fragrance on fragrance! Create a kinship
with the pure and reluctant rind,
with the juice that loads the ecstatic fruit!

But what can I dedicate to you, Master, say,
you who taught creatures how to hear?
My memory of one spring day,
and its evening, in Russia —, a horse . . .

A white stallion that roamed in my direction
from the village, a hobble on his fetlock,
out on the meadows for the night, alone;
how the shock of his mane bounced on his neck

in time with his high spirits — and with
the rhythm of his clumsy, shackled gallop.
How the wellsprings surged, blood of the stallion!

He could feel the expanses, that one!
How he neighed, how he listened — your myth
closed its circle in him.

His image — I offer it up.

But you now, whom I felt like a flower
I had no name for, you, taken away,
let me show you to them *once*, let me remember,
lovely playmate, unconquerable cry.

Dancer first, who suddenly, body filled with delay,
stood still, as if her youth were being cast
in bronze. Grieving and listening. Then, from high
agents, music fell into her changing heart.

Sickness drew near. Already possessed by shadows,
her blood rushed darkening, and yet, as if running
    scared,
it surged toward its natural springtide.

Again and again, though falls and darkness interrupted,
it glowed like the earth. Until after hideous blows
it ran through a gate that was hopelessly wide.

Breathing, you invisible poem!
Worldspace incessantly having its pure
traffic with our own being. Counterweight system
in which I rhythmically occur.

Lone wave, whose
gradual sea I am;
you sparsest of possible seas —
making room.

How many places in space have already
been inside me! Many a wind
is like a son to me . . .

Do you know me, air? You, full of places which
once were mine? You — once the smooth rind,
the roundness and leaf of my speech.

Mirrors: no one who knows has ever
described you, said what you're really like.
You who are filled with gaps of time
the way holes fill a sieve.

Spendthrifts in empty drawing rooms,
when evening arrives, deep as the woods . . .
like a sixteen-point stag, the faint shine roams
through your unreachable solitudes.

At times you seem filled with paintings.
Some seem to go straight into you — others
you've shyly sent away. Of course

the loveliest one will remain, until
there in those self-contained cheeks, clear
Narcissus, released, breaks in by force.

Oh this is the animal that never was.
They didn't know that, they just went ahead
and loved it; its walk, bearing, neck — they loved
even the light of its silent gaze.

Never existed. And yet, because they loved,
a pure creature began to occur. They always
left room for it, and in that cleared space
it simply lifted its head, and hardly needed

to exist. They never fed it grain
but rather, always, impossibility.
And that gave the animal such energy

that it grew a brow-horn. A single horn.
And it came white unto a virgin here —
and *was*, in the silver mirror, and in her.

Flower-muscle that unlocks, bit by bit,
the meadow-morning of the anemone,
until the polyphonic sky's loud light
pours down into her lap,

muscle of endless receptiveness
stretched in the quiet blossom-star,
so overcome, sometimes, by fullness,
that sundown's signal to rest

barely allows you to refurl
the overextended petals: you, the drive
and energy of how many worlds!

We violent ones last longer.
But *when*, in which of all our lives,
are we so open, such receivers?

Rose, growing throne of yourself, to the ancients
you were a chalice with a simple rim.
For us, you're the full, innumerable bloom,
the inexhaustible subject.

In your opulence you seem like clothing around clothing
around a body that's nothing more than brightness;
but your separate leaf is both the shunning
and the denial of every kind of dress.

For centuries your fragrance called across
its sweetest names to us; it's there
suddenly, hanging in the air like fame.

Still, we don't know what to call it. We guess . . .
and memory, summoned from hours we *could* name,
gives itself up to that fragrance once more.

Flowers, kinfolk at last to arranging hands,
(hands of young women, long ago and now), you
who lay on the garden table, often from rim to
rim, weary and mildly wounded

awaiting the water that would revive you
from death, already begun —, and now
lifted again between the streaming poles
of feeling fingers, that have even more power

to do good than you guessed, weightless ones,
when you came to in that jug, cooling slowly
and giving off the warmth of young women

like confessions, like thick, fatiguing sins
the act of plucking brought on, relating you again
to those who ally themselves with your blooming.

Be ahead of all partings, as if they were
behind you, like the winter that's just past.
For among the winters is one so endlessly winter
that your heart, if you overwinter, can survive it.

Be dead in Eurydice, always—, climb with more song,
climb with more praise, back up into pure relation.
Here in the kingdom of decay, among what's wasting,
be a tingling glass that shatters itself with sound.

Exist while you know the state of nonexistence,
the endless ground of your own deep pulse, so that
you can fulfill it completely this one time.

With the used-up, as well as the muffled and useless
stock of full nature, the unreckoned sum,
count yourself in, rejoicing, and then demolish the
        count.

Look at the flowers, loyal to the earth —
we lend them fate from fate's border, but
who knows if they regret the way they wither?
Maybe it's we who are their real regret.

All things want to float. And we go around like burdens,
settling ourselves on everything, ravished by weight;
what deadly teachers we are, when things in fact
have the gift of forever being children.

If someone took them into inmost sleep and slept
soundly with things — how lightly he might rise
changed, to changed days, from that communal depth.

Or maybe he'd stay; and they'd blossom and praise
him, the convert, now one with these brothers and
        sisters
all still in the midst of the winds and the meadows.

Oh fountain-mouth, giver, you never-tiring
mouth that says and says the same pure thing —
you marble mask, held up against
the water's streaming face. And in the distances

the aqueducts' descent. From far away,
from the Apennine slopes, passing graves,
they carry you your speech, which then
spills down the aging blackness of your chin

and falls into the basin there.
Basin: the sleeping, sidelong ear,
the marble ear in which you always speak.

One of the earth's ears. So that she's talking
just to herself. Push a pitcher in between,
she'll think you're interrupting.

Listen. You can hear harrows at work,
the first ones. Again, the human rhythms
in the hanging stillness of the rank
early-spring earth. What's coming seems

untasted, completely new. What
came to you so often seems now to
come the first time. You always expected it,
but you never took it. It took you.

Even leaves that hung on the oaks all winter
seem, in the evening, to be a future brown.
Sometimes the winds pass a signal around.

The thickets are black. But heaps of manure
are an even darker black in the pastures.
Every hour that goes by is younger.

Silent friend of many distances, feel
how your breath is enlarging space.
Among the rafters of dark belfries
let yourself ring. What preys on you will

strengthen from such nourishment.
Come and go with metamorphosis.
What's your most painful experience?
If what you drink's bitter, turn to wine.

In this huge night, become
the magic at the crossways of your senses.
Be what their strange encounter means.

And if the earthly forgets about you,
say to the quiet earth: I flow.
Speak to the rushing water — say: I am.

NOTES

The Book of Pictures does not represent Rilke's earliest work, but rather the work of his early maturity. As the dates indicate, it had more than one version and was added to over time. The "Nine Voices" sequence represents a late phase of this period, a move away from the more solitary, meditative and picturesque poems and into issues of social interaction that give a new dimension to Rilke's response to Symbolism.

The New Poems also represent work over a considerable period, and they divide into a first and second volume. "The Bowl of Roses" is the final poem in Volume One. My sequence reflects the order of appearance in both volumes.

The friend who is the subject of *Requiem* is the painter Paula Modersohn-Becker. She had died shortly after giving birth to a daughter, following a reconciliation with her husband, Otto Modersohn. He was a painter in the Worpswede group and wished to stay in Germany, while Paula needed to be in Paris to pursue her interest in French modernist painting. Adrienne Rich has conjectured in a poem ("Paula Becker to Clara Westhoff") that she did not want the child, and Rilke obviously feels too that the demands of marriage and motherhood created a deep conflict with the demands of art. Rilke's version of this, like Rich's, of course reflects his own biases, and the whole matter may be more complicated. Paula Becker' s paintings and drawings are full of nursing mothers and of mothers sleeping next to their babies. The experience of motherhood clearly fascinated her, and we need to remember that her death arose not from an art-life conflict but from a medical problem. With better care and recovered health, Paula Modersohn-Becker might well have continued her life both as a painter and as a mother.

My version of this poem introduces more frequent stanza-breaks than in the original.